SHOCKERS OF THE SEA

AND OTHER ELECTRIC ANIMALS

Caroline Arnold
Illustrated by Crista Forest

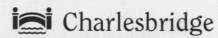 Charlesbridge

Text Copyright ©1999 by Caroline Arnold
Illustrations copyright © 1999 by Crista Forest

Published by Charlesbridge Publishing
85 Main Street
Watertown, MA 02472
(617) 926-0329
www.charlesbridge.com

Printed in South Korea
(hc) 10 9 8 7 6 5 4 3 2 1
(sc) 10 9 8 7 6 5 4 3 2 1

Library of Congress Cataloging-in-Publication Data
Arnold, Caroline
    Shockers of the Sea/ by Caroline Arnold;
illustrated by Crista Forest.
                    p.   cm.
Summary: Introduces fishes and other animals with
"electric senses" and explains how they produce, detect,
and use electricity to survive.
    ISBN 0-88106-873-X (reinforced for library use)
    ISBN 0-88106-874-8 (softcover)
    1. Electric fishes–Juvenile literature. [1. Electric fishes.]
I. Forest, Crista, ill. II. Title.
QL639.1.A77   1999
597-dc21   98-7035
                                            CIP
                                            AC

The illustrations in this book were done in oil paint on canvas.
The display type and text type were set in Bodega and Leawood by Paige Davis.
Color separations were made by Eastern Rainbow.
Printed and bound by Sung In Printing, Inc.
Production supervision by Brian G. Walker
Designed by Rosanne Kakos-Main

A SHOCKING EXPERIENCE

Nearly two hundred years ago a scientist from Germany named Alexander von Humboldt went to the Amazon jungle. There, in a small pool, he found dozens of long, thin fish swimming in the muddy water. Von Humboldt watched one of them approach a smaller fish. ZAP! It sent out a giant burst of electricity and stunned the small fish. Then it easily caught the fish and ate it.

The long, thin fish was an electric eel. This kind of fish has the amazing ability to make and feel electricity. It has an electric sense. Many other kinds of fish have an electric sense, too. It helps them to survive.

Alexander von Humboldt explored in South America between 1799 and 1804. To study the eel, he touched one with his foot. ZAP! He felt a mighty shock. His leg hurt for the rest of the day. He was the first European to study electric eels in their natural home.

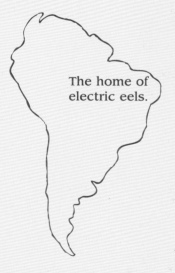

The home of electric eels.

A SIXTH SENSE

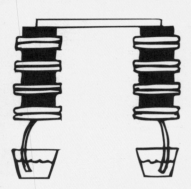

Volta's battery

Three hundred years ago scientists began to study electricity. The first electric battery was made in 1800 by an Italian scientist, Alessandro Volta. He modeled it on the electric organ of the ray, an electric fish that lives in the sea.

An electric eel is a strongly electric fish.

All knife fish, including these two species, can make and feel electricity. They are weakly electric fish.

The electric sense is as different from any of our senses as our senses are from one another. Our senses are seeing, hearing, smelling, tasting, and touching. Electric fish have one more. They can make and feel electricity.

Some species of fish have special organs in their bodies that make electricity. Others have special organs that can feel electricity. Some have both. All of these fish have the electric sense.

The strongly electric fish make so much electricity that you feel a shock if you touch them or get close to them. People cannot feel the tiny amount of electricity produced by weakly electric fish. Fish that can feel electricity are able to detect even very small amounts of it in the water.

Fish use their electric sense in many ways. The electric sense may help a fish get food, defend itself, locate hidden objects, find its way around in the water, or in some cases, "talk" to other fish.

The electric organ of a knife fish can make only three-tenths of a volt of electricity or less.

Making Electricity

The part of the body that makes the electricity is called an electric organ. The electric organ is a living battery. It is made of many tiny living cells. Each one makes a little electricity. Together they can make enough to produce a shock. Some fish that make electricity can turn it on and off in the same way that you push a switch to turn on and off the batteries of a flashlight. Some can also change their electric signal in the same way that you can turn a radio dial to change stations.

In many fish the electric organ is in the tail. But sometimes it is in the fish's head or under its skin. The size and shape of the electric organ vary in different species of fish.

An electric eel's powerful electric organ can produce a shock of up to six hundred volts. That's two thousand times stronger than the amount of electricity made by the knife fish.

The pinkish electric organ appears here in an "x-ray" view.

Feeling Electricity

Electric fish feel electricity in the water through special sense organs in their skin. These are called electric receptors. Almost all fish with electric organs also have electric receptors.

You, too, can feel electricity when you get an electric shock. The electricity hurts you, and you feel pain. But you do not have electric receptors or electric organs. People do not have an electric sense.

No one can "see" an electric field. The glow around these fish shows where the field would be.

A knife fish zeroes in on other fish with the help of its electric sense.

All animals, however, have small amounts of electricity in their bodies, made by their nerves and muscles. Some of this electricity "leaks out" and surrounds the body with a kind of invisible halo of electricity. This is called an electric field. Fish with electric receptors can feel the electric fields of other fish and animals in the water. They can also feel electric impulses produced by other electric fish. Water is a good conductor of electricity. Electricity passes through water almost as easily as it travels through wires into your house.

The electric receptors on a fish are arranged in lines and patterns up and down its body. The fish uses them to sense electricity over its entire body.

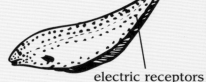

electric receptors

*M*any electric fish can swim backward as well as forward, by rippling their long fins. Their electric sense helps them know where to go. They do not need to use their eyes, though some of them can see well, too.

Finding Their Way with Electricity

Just as you can hear yourself when you talk, fish with electric organs and electric receptors can feel their own electricity. When a fish has its electric organ on, electricity flows through the water and surrounds it. This creates an electric field around the fish. This field is only a fraction of a volt strong. If there is a rock, fish, or other object nearby, that object makes an invisible electric "shadow" on the fish's skin. The fish "feels" the shadow with its electric receptors and uses this information to find out the shape and size of the object.

Electric fields do not really glow. But they do help fish detect nearby objects.

The ability to "feel" objects in the water with electricity is called electrolocation. It is something like having a built-in radar system that works with electricity. Many electric fish are active at night and many live in muddy water. Electrolocation makes it easy for a fish to find its way when it is hard to see.

STRONGLY ELECTRIC FISH

Strongly electric fish make so much electricity that their shocks are painful or even dangerous.

They use their electricity to defend themselves. Animals that might want to harm them stay away because they do not want to be shocked. Strongly electric fish also use their electricity to get food. Their shocks are strong enough to stun or kill the small animals that they eat.

Electric Eels

Electric eels are the most powerful of all electric fish. A large eel can make shocks of up to six hundred volts of electricity! The eel only turns on its electricity for a fraction of a second at a time. Most of the time the eel's large electric organ is turned off. The eel turns it on when it is hunting for food, and it can make up to 150 shocks per hour. Each shock is strong but lasts only an instant.

An electric eel has two small electric organs in addition to its large one. It uses the small electric organs for electrolocation.

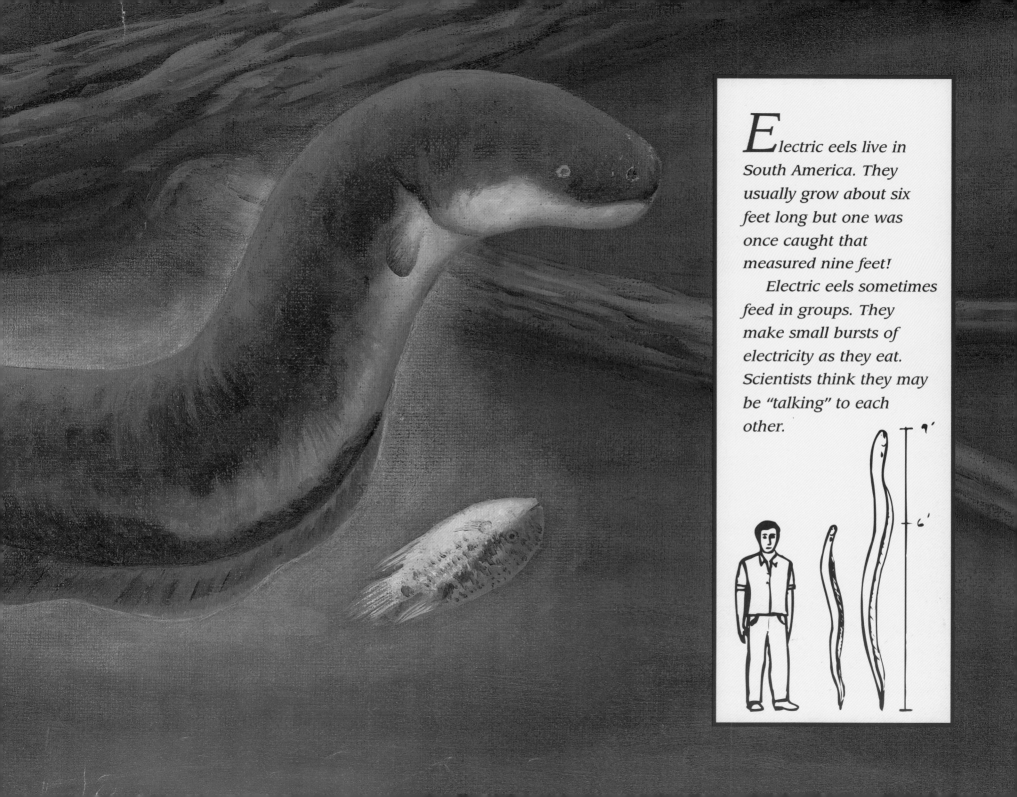

*E*lectric eels live in South America. They usually grow about six feet long but one was once caught that measured nine feet!

Electric eels sometimes feed in groups. They make small bursts of electricity as they eat. Scientists think they may be "talking" to each other.

9'

6'

Electric Catfish

Electric catfish live in the lakes and rivers of Africa, including the Nile River. These large fish are not fussy and will eat almost anything that they can find. Electric catfish shock their prey and then catch it. They do most of their eating at night. Sometimes a fisherman catches an electric catfish in his net along with other fish. But when he touches the wet net the shock is so strong that he drops all the fish back into the river.

Recently scientists discovered three more species of African catfish with electric organs. These fish make only small amounts of electricity and do so only when fighting each other.

Catfish have long, catlike whiskers on their snouts. Many kinds of catfish live all over the world, but only this one can give you a strong shock. The electric catfish is the second most powerful of all electric fish and makes shocks that can be as strong as 350 volts. Some electric catfish grow to be more than three feet long.

Electric Rays

Rays are large, flat fish that live in the ocean. They glide through the water by rippling the sides of their bodies like giant wings. There are about three hundred species of rays. Of these, more than thirty are electric. The biggest electric rays are five feet long and the smallest are only seventeen inches. The famous manta rays and stingrays are not electric.

An electric ray has one large electric organ on each side of its head. It can make as much as two hundred volts of electricity. Rays usually eat fish, crabs, shrimp, and other small sea animals. An electric ray pounces on its victim, wraps it in its fins, and shocks it before eating it.

Thousands of years ago people in ancient Greece and Rome used electric rays as painkillers. A patient with a headache stood on a live electric ray or wrapped one around his or her head. Sometimes the shock cured the headache. Can you imagine having a ray wrapped around your head?

Pictures of electric rays were painted on pottery in ancient Greece.

Stargazers

Stargazers can make about fifty volts of electricity. Their electric organs are behind their eyes. A stargazer does not use electricity to catch its prey. Instead it buries itself at the bottom of the sea and peeks out of the sand. When a crab or a small fish comes by, the stargazer snaps it up. Scientists think that stargazers may use their electricity to subdue their prey after they catch it.

There are more than twenty kinds of stargazers. The biggest are only about sixteen inches long.

There are more than one hundred kinds of skates. Some grow to be eight feet long.

Skates

Skates are ocean fish with small electric organs in their tails. They are the weakest of the strongly electric fish and can only make about four volts of electricity. That is not enough to stun even a small fish.

Scientists do not know how skates use their electricity. Maybe they use it to find food. Maybe they use it to communicate with each other and find mates. Scientists are studying skates to find out more about them.

WEAKLY ELECTRIC FISH

Gymnarchus (jim-nar-kus) is a fish that cannot see very well. Yet when it swims around in a river or in a fish tank it rarely bumps into anything. One scientist who studied this fish wanted to find out why. He put two flowerpots into a tank with a gymnarchus and hid a piece of food behind each one. One pot was filled with a material that conducted electricity and the other was not. The fish learned to find food behind the first pot. That showed that the fish was using its electric sense to find the food.

The tiny electric organ of a weakly electric fish makes such a small amount of electricity—less than one volt—that it takes special machines to measure it. Some of these machines change the fish's electric signals to sounds we can hear. Each kind of fish has its own electric signal or "voice." These voices vary from chirps and trills to clicks and rumbles.

Weakly electric fish have their electric organs turned on most of the time. The electric organs of strongly electric fish, on the other hand, are usually turned off. They produce electricity only in short, sudden bursts.

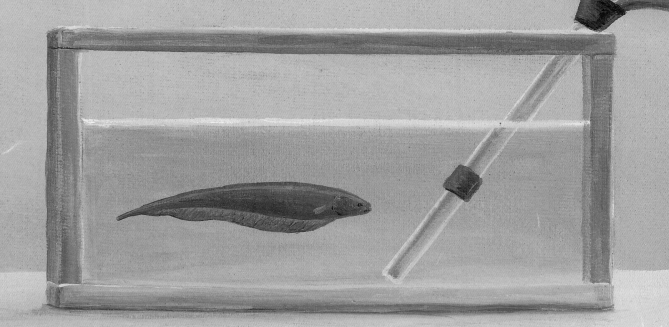

The gymnarchus is found in the Nile River and in the lakes and streams of West Africa. It swims by rippling the long fin along its back.

The snout fish lives in Africa. It is sometimes called an elephant-nose fish or baby whale. The snout fish has a long snout that it uses when rooting around for food on the bottoms of streams and ponds.

Most weakly electric fish live in shallow water. During the day they hide under banks, behind rocks, or among tree roots. At night they swim out into the main part of the stream or pond and look for food. They do not need to see because they can find their way electrically. There are more than two hundred kinds of weakly electric fish.

"Talking" with Electricity

Perhaps the most amazing discovery about weakly electric fish is that they use electric signals to "talk" to each other. They use electric messages to tell each other who they are, where they are, whether they want to mate, and other things they need to communicate.

Most of the enemies of these electric fish cannot feel electric impulses. So the weakly electric fish can "talk" to each other secretly and safely even when there are other fish around.

Some of the strongly electric fish may use electricity to communicate with each other.

Here are some of the things that weakly electric fish say:

This is what kind of fish I am.
I am a male   *or*
I am a female.
Watch out! I'm going to fight you.
Please don't fight me.
I'm leaving.
Come join the group.
I'm ready to mate.

FISH THAT CAN "FEEL" ELECTRICITY

*C*atfish, paddlefish, ratfish, reedfish, lampreys, lungfish, sturgeons, and the coelacanth (see-la-kanth) are among more than two hundred species of fish that have the ability to feel electricity.

lamprey

All sharks and rays are able to "feel" electricity. They cannot make electricity, but they have electric receptors in their skin. Electric receptors provide them with important information about their surroundings. They use their receptors to detect amounts of electricity millions of times smaller than what people can feel.

Dogfish are a kind of small shark. They search the ocean floor for flatfish hiding in the sand. Even if a flatfish is totally covered a dogfish can find it by sensing its electric field. Then the shark digs up the flatfish and eats it.

A mako shark cruises in deep water hunting for prey.

ARE FISH THE ONLY ONES?

Besides fish a few other animals are known to have an electric sense. Their electric receptors seem to help them find food.

Echidna (ih-kid-nuh): This egg-laying mammal lives in Australia and New Guinea. It eats ants and other insects that it finds in the damp soil of the forest floor.

Platypus: This egg-laying mammal from Australia feeds at night along the bottoms of streams. It can find worms and other food even in total darkness.

Giant salamanders: These giant amphibians live in China and Japan. They can grow to be six feet long. They live in or near water their whole lives and eat small aquatic animals.

Axolotl (ax-suh-lot-ul): This mole salamander lives in Mexico and the western United States. It lives in water and eats insects and other small animals.

A SPECIAL SENSE

The ability to make and feel electricity helps fish and other animals survive in a damp or watery world. For fish with large electric organs electricity is a powerful weapon to use in defense or to capture prey. For fish with small electric organs electricity helps them find their way around and gives them a special way to communicate with one another. And for animals that can feel electricity the electric sense helps them find food and gives them important information about their environment. Scientists are only beginning to learn about the amazing ways that fish and other animals use their electric sense. We can only imagine what it might be like to have an electric sense. To us it almost seems to be magic.

You will probably never see an electric fish in its natural home. But you can see electric fish in many public aquariums.

GLOSSARY

amphibian . . . . an animal that is able to live both on land and in water

electric field . . . . a kind of invisible electric "halo" or "cloud" surrounding any source of electricity

electric organ . . . . a body organ capable of producing electricity

electric receptor . . . . a part of the body able to detect even small amounts of electricity

electric sense . . . . having special organs in the body that can either produce or feel electricity

electrolocation. . . . . using electricity to "feel" objects in the water

fish . . . . an animal that lives entirely in water and breathes through gills that get oxygen from the water

mammal. . . . . an animal that has fur or hair and feeds milk to its young

prey . . . . animals that are hunted for food

species . . . . a group of plants or animals that share similar characteristics and can interbreed

volt . . . . a unit of measurement for electric potential named in honor of Alessandro Volta

---

Web Resources:

Maler, Leonard. "Electric Fish Primer." University of Ottawa.
http://aix1.uottawa.ca/~nberman/primer.html. Information and links.

Assad, Chris and Brian Rasnow. "Electric Fish." California Institute of Technology.
http://www.bbb.caltech.edu/bowerlab/ElectricFish/index.html
(Feb. 13, 1997). Good links to movies and simulations as well as information.

Author Unknown. "HHMI's 1997 Holiday Lectures on Science/Neurobiology." Howard Hughes Medical Institute.
http://www.hhmi.org/grants/lectures/97lect/electro (1997). See a simulation of an electric field.

Author Unknown. "The Senses of Fish." Sea World/Busch Gardens.
http://www.seaworld.org/Fishes/senses.html (1996). The electric sense and other senses.

Thanks to the following for help and advice: Carl Hopkins, Cornell University; Leonard Maler, University of Ottawa; Mark Nelson, The Beckman Institute, University of Illinois; Brian Rasnow, formerly of the California Institute of Technology; Phillip Stoddard, Florida International University; and Harold Zakon, Institute for Neuroscience, University of Texas.